MW00965075

Breccia

Breccia

haiku and related forms

Irene Golas

Ignatius Fay

Copyright 2012 © Irene Golas and Ignatius Fay

All rights reserved.

No part of this book may be reproduced in any form or by any electronic or mechanical means, including all information storage and retrieval systems, without written permission from the author.

Reviewers may quote brief passages in review.

Copyright of individual poems is retained by the author.

Library and Archives Canada Cataloguing in Publication

Golas, Irene H., 1955-
    Breccia : haiku and related forms / Irene Golas, Ignatius Fay.

ISBN 978-0-9809572-2-8

    1. Haiku, Canadian (English). 2. Sudbury (Ont.)--Poetry.
3. Mines and mineral resources--Ontario--Sudbury--Poetry.
I. Fay, Ignatius, 1950- II. Title.

PS8613.O48B74 2012   C811'.6   C2012-904586-1

Design by: Irene Golas and Ignatius Fay

Layout by: Ignatius Fay

Published by: Ignatius Fay, Irene Golas and Lulu.com

Copies of this work may be purchased online at: http://www.lulu.com/shop/ignatius-fay-and-irene-golas/breccia/paperback/product-20348192.html

Jocelyne Villeneuve (1941-1998),
respected Sudbury author and poet

introduced Ignatius to haiku and encouraged
his efforts until her death

an early source of inspiration to Irene

Contents

Introduction

A breccia is a rock composed of angular fragments of preexisting rocks embedded in a fine-grained matrix or cement. The fragments were produced by forces such as erosion, impact or volcanic activity. The Sudbury Breccia was formed by the impact of a large meteorite about 1.85 billion years ago. It is associated with most of the area's rich nickel-iron-copper ore bodies.

We chose *Breccia* as our title to reflect the nature of the collection and our geographical location in Sudbury, Ontario, Canada. We were struck by the similarity between this collection and that rock type. After selecting published and unpublished haiku, senryu, tanka and haibun, we arranged them in a way that produced a unique new whole—a poetic breccia.

One section of this book, "Sudbury Breccia," grew out of a few poems about that northern mining town. We were attracted to the idea of examining life in such a town from World War II into the new millennium as seen through the eyes of a haiku poet.

The diverse cultural mix of the miners themselves further enhances the breccia theme. The earliest miners were, primarily, a mélange of European immigrants who relocated to find a better life. This potpourri was enriched by large numbers of immigrants and displaced persons fleeing a war-ravaged Europe. The result was a northern Ontario mining culture with a distinctly varied foundation.

We decided to integrate our poems, creating several extended sequences in which each poem suggests some relationship to the immediately preceding poem. The degree to which we succeeded will be judged by the reader.

To identify our poems in this organic flow, we chose two different but complementary fonts:

Poems by Irene are in the font Present

Poems by Ignatius are in the font Ruzicka Freehand LT Std.

Haiku / Senryu
I

first cicada…
a feeling of something running out

jar of skin creme —
the chuckle of dry leaves
on the patio

shorter days —
opting to use her
antique teacups

a row of teddies
on the old lady's bed
visiting hours

after many years
a friendship renewed —
packet of seeds

turning the garden
    releasing
        winter's final darkness

first robin
the suck of garden mud
on rubber boots

parsley
so green I hear it
spring rain

muddy boot prints —
after-school bouquet
of pussy willows

postpartum:
I leave the hospital
cradling flowers

hummingbird
on invisible wings
then gone

heat wave
the redness of
geraniums

heavy wheeze
coughing red on the snow
— pallbearer

sand ripples...
what to do with dad's ashes

his urn
half-full of loose change
April drizzle

just enough distance
between the hearse and me
mother's funeral

May predawn
the rapture of being
— obituary

black & white photos…
no clues as to who
mother really was

moonless —
camp dock adrift between
Milky Ways

blackout
children discover
the stars

the shared darkness
of a power outage…
nothing to say

ice pellets
dad speaks his mind

poetry night
my words from her lips —
honeysuckle buds

steady rain...
settling deeper
into poetry

cold and still...
the sound of
falling shadows

the dog's shadow
over half the road —
winter solstice

explaining bluegrass
while she bathes me
snow squall warning

no blizzard
the boys settle for
a pillow fight

shooting baskets
the boys discuss what's gay
what isn't

writers' circle...
noticed for wearing
men's shirts

riverside park
its coat of many colors
tattered by the wind

blustery day
the north wind and I
compete for my breath

a chipmunk
noses around
my oxygen tank

cool fingertips
soft against my inner wrist
she measures my life

home again —
I wash off the smell
of hospital soap

morning stiffness —
freshly cut tulips
on the drain board

every step through creaking snow
the arthritic feet

growing deaf...
if only I could lip-read
the sparrow's song

so much to be said
too much left unsaid —
shared bran muffin

after
the funeral...
chocolate ice cream

summer evening
a clean t-shirt shares
my frozen yoghurt

hanging laundry:
she turns underwear
to hide the holes

cool March breeze —
between faded tea towels
her frayed pink bra

second honeymoon
the power of Niagara
somewhat diminished

idling tour bus
the driver alone with
stock market quotes

pension courtyard
an old woman airs shoes
on a windowsill

sirocco wind
mossy granite boulders
of the farmhouse walls

ripening barley
the whistle of a groundhog
pierces the heat

brown shadows
silent among the dark pines
wapiti

gunshot slap
of a beaver's tail
splitting firewood

hunter's moon —
he saves the smallest apples
for the deer

a case of beer
the only thing killed
moose tag

smeared windshield —
newly deceased grasshoppers
after the swarm

mother's funeral...
the prickle of wings
between my shoulders

under the eaves
an empty swallows' nest —
unexpected tears

empty nest
gleefully she prepares
curries and tofu

barszcz and rye bread...
the rough hands
of the soldiers

Barszcz is a Polish beetroot soup, often made with other vegetables and usually served with sour cream.

her brother's hug
the arm he didn't leave
in Afghanistan

about the war...
mother simply stares
into her soup

brown-bag lunch
a chipmunk freezes head down
on the tree trunk

bone scan —
autumn mist blurs
the pines

diagnosis
longest day of my life
— winter solstice

more snow...
will dad see
another spring

Day of the Dead
dad's advice is no better
since his death

fifty-fifth year...
wishing motherhood
was a hundred-yard dash

Stanley Cup game
relacing his old ball glove
for his daughter

girls vs. boys
quietly a hockey mom
cheers for the girls

Valentine's Day
my daughter's delicate
butterfly kisses

overnight
blossoms on the crabapple
my daughter's sixteen

graduation
chiffon, a pink corsage
one angry zit

her biking gloves
on the bloody ER floor...
donor card

moss-covered rocks...
mother never talks about
the one that died

van windows
fogged with our breath
— arguing God

long haul trucker
himself a heavy load
rain to snow

Greyhound west…
we doze in and out
of life stories

Europe by train...
poppies on the way
to Dachau

white on green
endless rows of crosses
list of MIAs

newly found cousin...
tongue-tied
in my mother tongue

worlds apart —
two river-worn pebbles
in my palm

by lamplight
braiding new mooring ropes
his big tanned hands

summer evening...
grandpa on the front step
rolling smokes

after sundown
against the harvester —
blowin' blues harp

summerfest
young country singer
aw-shucks and twang

blazing sun
farm buildings a tumble
of wooden blocks

hurricane
stairs to a second floor
no longer there

dementia ward
all day mother tries all day
the doors to open doors

a winged ant
trapped between the doors —
ultimatum

small nail hole
where her picture hung
Easter with the girls

boxes of photos...
taken when I was sure
they would mean something

absences
the soft pink center
of the white orchid

broken promises
a thistle takes root
in mother's heart

night fog
thinking about wrong turns
I make one

table for one
will I ever learn to keep
my mouth shut

autumn rain...
the springs in the old love seat

knees and floorboards
cold and creaking —
new year

on the wall
behind the icicles
rainbows

first warm day
father gets out
his cap and cane

maple syrup
in her voice
mud on the carpet

first cattails —
the splash swallows
the leaping trout

dusk
aware of my heartbeat…
the crickets

Tattoo Poems
Haiku / Senryu / Tanka

choosing a design
for our family tattoo
February thaw

pretattoo
shaving my thigh
in the sauna

awaiting my ride
to the tattoo parlor
light frost

lowering weight
of fall's purple sky
tattoo needle

across her back
the tattoo artist draws
the rustle of dry leaves

tattoo
on her lower back
the air blue

buzz and sting
of the tattoo needle
discussing Christmas

winter tires —
trying not to scratch
the itchy tattoo

new year, new ink
the tattoo artist's
red dragon logo

three elderly ladies
comparing tattoos
snow clouds

her iris tattoo
she thinks my crinoid
is also a plant

A *crinoid* is a marine animal that looks surprisingly like a plant. It is related to starfish and sand dollars. Very common as fossils, only a few species survive today.

tattoo parlor
teen girls and body art
what bikini line

arraignment
listing her offenses
teddy bear tattoo

dreaming
of her chopped Indian…
full-back tattoo

The *Indian,* debuting in 1901, is the oldest American brand of motorcycles. A *chopped* motorcyle, or 'chopper,' is a modified stock motorcycle. Typically, it has a longer frame with a stretch front end, further extended by a longer fork.

new tattoo —
applying balm to my thigh
summer ends

perfect day
blue sky, August sun
wanting to run
up the street shouting
look at my new tattoo

bees wax balm
on the new tattoo
my full-thigh
can't hold a candle
to my daughter's full-back

the mosaic
of windblown leaves
grows on her back

tattoo artists
doing each other's back
the shortest day

purple hair
piercings, tattoos, leather
— snowball fight

her fingers
warm from the teacup
stroke my tattoo

furnace repair...
planning our next tattoo
by email

Canada Day Fireworks
A Haiku Sequence

July First
kids and fire crackers
the shed in flames

summer night
firemen silhouetted
by the orange roar

deck smells
barbecued spareribs
and burning shingles

melted vinyl
frozen in giant drips
lemonade break

sweltering
men assemble to raze
the garbage shed

slick with sweat
t-shirt glued to his back
he swings his hammer

summer sun
making short work of the shed
they stop for beer

cement workers
drinking from the hose
new walls in two days

six a.m.
mixer, gofer, bricklayer
barechested and tan

heat wave
the roofers singing
Italian opera

Haiku / Senryu

II

facial bruises
the color of raw liver
poinsettias

supper late
his temper can't make
the pots boil faster

her German Shepherd
watching every move —
rage of fall colors

flannel p.j.s
explaining the divorce
to young daughters

ex-wife's partner
dead in his sleep
more snow

hearse and two limos
over a bridge and gone —
Christmas Eve

hearts & flowers...
putting back
the Valentine cards

cross-tie walking
creosote in the hot sun
talking about girls

teenage girls
wearing mostly attitude —
warm summer breeze

lilac on the breeze…
missing the bounce
of my ponytail

strands of hair
on her sweaty neck
low-fat breakfast

homeless man
asleep out of the wind
late for Pilates

on the breeze...
bracing scent of my neighbor's
shower gel

windblown leaves —
the squeak of her runners
as she damp mops

autumn wind –
the old woman tries to hold
her tremor

naked aspens
shivering at sunset
– dressed to dine out

Christmas Eve –
all I want is you
without long johns

dancing sugar plums –
just enough cookie crumbs
to be convincing

too normal
the act of brewing tea
waiting for word

cancer...
delicate curves
of the kidney bowl

cheap silver neck chain
the first thing I gave her
palliative care

Remembrance Day
reading her old letters
and wondering

note from mom
so proud of her boy
September obit

days grow short
the paperboy one house
ahead of dusk

Christmas Day
aunts in the kitchen
sharing cooking secrets

home for Christmas
mother's calendar still turned
to summer

skinny-dipping among
stars trapped in the river
— little white lie

candlelight
the glint of beach sand
in her cleavage

left breast gone
the one my infant son
preferred

lamplight
the soft curve of her breast
in absentia

April morning
reading on the floor
in the sunny spot

box of crayons
trying so hard to stay
within the lines

crayon bunnies
join the fridge dinosaurs
wild irises

early sun
brook trout jumping
circle to circle

summer shower
kids laughing
in the sprinkler

cumulus clouds...
voices of berry pickers
drift across the field

pick-it-yourself
filling six-quart baskets
and their faces

farmers' market –
the sour old woman
selling honey

through her reflection
in the windshield
fields of harvesters

cold prairie night
freight train tunnels the sound
of its whistle

despite the snow
coldest day of the year
silent treatment

homemade wine
dad's friends turn up
the volume

reggae music
from open patio doors —
soft April rain

table set for one
red grapefruit on bone china
sounds from a yard sale

spaces
in my address book
November rain

cheery bouquet
wildflowers handpicked
for her...by her

flu season —
her birthday roses
outlast the romance

a second look
at a second-rate novel...
down with the flu

office picnic
my book returned
dog-eared and scuffed

the paperback
a mass of unglued pages —
evening sauna

empathy
for the lobster —
hot tub

smokehouse embers...
the sweetness
of new potatoes

shoofly pie —
down here I'm the one
with the accent

spring flamingos
standing on one leg
making 4s

neon jellyfish
pulsating on the strand
—barefoot at low tide

on vacation…
my tomatoes call
every day

lobster traps
stacked in the shore grass
—salt-gnarled fingers

from his bar stool
the café owner's dog
sizes us up

the dog and I
on the moonlit dock
scratching bug bites

bumper to bumper
leaving cottage country
summer romance

the fetus kicks just twice...
end of summer

orange asters —
Harley's chrome glinting
in the brief sun

her aging skin
the texture of dried apples
— fresh gourds for sale

autumn sunset —
grandma's fingers stained
with beet juice

dad's firm handshake
increasingly frail —
ides of March

weathered old man
gnarled as his walking stick —
handful of daisies

some nights
he turns his face away
man in the moon

darkness and lilacs —
we work on a crossword
over the phone

spring moon
new phases
my teen daughter

her spring haircut —
rapping the pickle jar lid
with a knife

sudden shower —
the boys dash out
without shoes

rain day at camp
vintage Archie comics
read and reread

white butts
stark against deep tans
catching crayfish

a satellite dish
on every balcony
empty ball field

crunch of snow —
unknown neighbors
hang a Christmas star

deep red cranberries
shriveled on the bush
— dose of Viagra

mid-January —
avoiding eye contact
with his gay brother

tax form
writing where it says
office use only

three a.m.
summer wind, sixties rock
the open road

nursing home —
father no longer looks
out the window

dried forget-me-nots
among my keepsakes
from whom

fitting a blue piece
to dad's jigsaw puzzle
— Groundhog Day

long johns
in the shape of me —
end of winter

brows furrowed
dad eyes my Dali
Easter Vigil

morphine
the day drifts
have I eaten

Alzheimer's cloud
his head pokes out briefly
dad again

arrhythmia
one more health issue —
hummingbirds

basting the turkey —
her breasts, her great vanity
riddled with cancer

meteor shower
the small safety pin
on her bra strap

hot night
not a cool side
to the pillow

grapefruit segments
splayed like a pinwheel
early sunrise

the dilemma
where to submit her poems —
jar of grape jelly

gunmetal blue
hunting vest orange
all the fall colors

snow falling…
a darker silence
in father's room

Sudbury Breccia

A *breccia* is a rock composed of angular fragments of preexisting rocks embedded in a fine-grained matrix or cement. The fragments were produced by forces such as erosion, impact or volcanic activity. The Sudbury Breccia was formed by the impact of a large meteorite about 1.85 billion years ago. It is associated with most of the area's rich nickel-iron-copper ore bodies.

bush, rocks and water...
my immigrant mother
aghast at the train window

impact breccia —
foreign accents
in the miners' bunkhouse

growing family...
they wait for the company
to assign a house

mother's photo
in the INCO Triangle...
ESL class

INCO stands for International Nickel Company, the major corporation involved in the nickel mining industry around Sudbury, 1902–2006.

graveyard shift
getting home to the lament
of mourning doves

nickel town...
the tang of sulphur
on the breeze

smelter smokestacks
clouding the blue sky
ducklings in step

gray
among blackened rock
dead saplings

bone-snapping cold
this morning the car insists
on square tires

depths of the mine
a perpetual heat wave
sharing Christmas cake

Christmas
the stack stands plumeless
miners' first strike

mom and dad whisper
the miner who shot himself
week before Christmas

company & union
dad takes off
for the tobacco farms

asking dad
what a scab worker is...
snow to shovel

Lipton soup
bologna sandwiches
strike pay

the priest's sermon
on Palm Sunday
the strike continues

cottage industry
making wood-burning stoves
on company time

home workshop
tools from the mine
via lunch pail

across town
the mine's shift change horn —
stealing third

displaced person
the brown paper bag
as he leaves the mine

ears to the rails
waiting
for the ore train

throat-searing heat
molten slag reddens the night
but no mosquitoes

dog days
four o'clock ore train
counting the cars

his calves kept bald
by chafing rubber boots
no snow underground

rolling cigarettes
before leaving for the mine
hockey scores

packing his lunch pail
the Happy Gang
on the radio

breakfast of porridge
while dad eats his supper
graveyard shift

the mine's horn
signals an accident
fried chicken grows cold

the impact crack
on his miner's hat
new peach preserves

dressed for Easter Mass
the dent in his brush cut
from the miner's hat

patching overalls
the reek of Jiffy Sew
hangs on the fall air

new oil furnace
my first real kiss
in the coal bin

basement clothesline
dad's gray wool work socks
smell of furnace oil

the sweat-polished liner
of dad's mining hat
pillowcase for treats

trick or treat
yet another group
dressed as miners

hues of rust
on headframe and maples…
squeal of the hoist

last game
of the World Series
late for the cage

A *headframe* is the tall structure that houses the hoisting mechanism above a mine shaft.

A *cage* was a rough-hewn elevator compartment used to lower men, equipment and machinery into the mine. It had no ceiling, and its walls and gate were made of widely spaced wooden planks. Modern cages are similar in design, but made of steel or aluminum.

company Christmas
a gift for every kid...
home with pneumonia

curling
before going underground
at midnight

my long johns
on the basement clothesline
dwarfed by dad's

the talk at supper
Jacklegs, raise bore drills
and drifts without snow

three-shift schedule
Dominion Day weekend
lost to the short change

young miners brag
of sleeping in a drift
after the beach

A *Jackleg* is the trademark name of a compressed air drill used to bore holes into hard rock. The air leg acts as a partial support, making the job easier for the drill operator.

A *raise borer* or *raise bore drill* is a machine used to excavate a circular shaft between two levels of a mine without the use of explosives. A small hole is drilled by conventional means from the upper level to the lower. Then a huge bit is pulled upward, or raised, from the lower level to the upper.

A *drift* is a horizontal or inclined mine passage that branches off the main tunnel in order to follow a mineral vein.

Levack North Mine
sixteen hundred feet
comparing sunburns

'in the mood'
written on his lunch pail...
girls in shorts

summer afternoon
using the ore train
to flatten pennies

hiding in tall grass —
the penny shakes off the rail
before the ore train

home to his son
samples of breccia
picnic at the lake

dad's St. Christopher
black with sweat
and mine dust

miner's glasses
outlined on his grimy face
Labor Day weekend

back to school
yellow notepads smuggled home
in dad's lunch pail

first week
a mining accident pulls
a friend from class

two p.m.
the school shudders
with the mine's daily blast

hard hat in hand
dad singing 'El Paso'...
fresh pumpkin pie

lunch pail
on the back porch step
busted bicycle

crabapples
and a dog-eared Zane Grey
in his lunch pail

predawn snow
twenty men lowered
into pitch black

the cage bounces
with the miners' weight
a stomach growls

headlamps off
inky black and the sounds
of shifting rock

in the dark basement
playing with his headlamp
feet numb from hockey

harsh winter —
weary miners lobbied
by a new union

slushy sidewalk
union organizers
pass out handbills

dad and my uncle
argue union politics
homemade donuts

dad praying —
fear of Commie influence
on the union merger

home through the snow
after the union rally
telling mom he's scared

bloodied snow —
dad stops going
to union meetings

late night knock
a friend hurt at the rally
snow-wet slippers

union riot
cops and miners crowd
the ER

in the snowy street
a crushed black lunch pail
police siren

biking to work
Chiquita banana stickers
cover his lunch pail

the special status
of drillers on bonus
April Fool's trick

moving day
his father's job lost
to a Scooptram

retired from mining
the school janitor's limp
worse in autumn

A *Scooptram* is a piece of heavy equipment used primarily underground for moving loose
rock, ore, etc. Similar to a front-end loader, it has a much lower profile and is jointed in the
center in order to move around in tight spaces.

a poisoned fox
in the tailings pond
rains of April

played-out mine site —
the green of young thistles
in rust-stained soil

Junction Creek
silt slowly fills
a shopping cart

Tailings are a mixture of water and finely ground rock left after the useful minerals have been removed at a smelter. They are permanently stored in depressions, often natural, or small bodies of water called *tailings ponds*.

whacking
a dead sapling...
whiff of sulphur

regreening...
new poplar saplings to screen
the tailings pond

pine seedlings
in the old nickel mine
scarred landscape

sunset silhouettes
the old mine's head frame —
new growth forest

new to Sudbury
the repeated question...
so, how do you like it?

the growing impact
of three mining deaths
shatter cones

impact craters
astronauts-in-training
study the breccia

Shatter cones are cone- or fan-shaped features in rocks, with radiating fracture lines. They are formed when rocks are subjected to shock waves from any significant impact, size being related to the intensity and proximity of the impact. They range from a few centimeters to more than five meters in length.

learning to map
the Sudbury Breccia
black flies

bookends
from Sudbury's breccia
spring fundraiser

summer shutdown
the smoke-free smelter stack
above blackened rocks

the earth rumbles
INCO blasting
or a developer?

blasting horn
blackened rocks give way
to big box stores

no more blueberries...
a black bear
on garbage night

lavender-pink and gold
Superstack's plume drifts
towards cottage country

The *Superstack,* at 1250 ft., is the second tallest free-standing smokestack in the world.
It was built in 1972 at INCO's Copper Cliff smelter to disperse sulphur dioxide and other
byproducts of the smelting process away from the city of Sudbury.

going underground
to study the cosmos
neutrino lab*

four thousand feet
into the breccia...
a trout hatchery

*This poem is a collaborative effort.

Breccia Tanka

Levack North Mine
sixteen-hundred-foot level
the weight
of three billion years
over my head

miners
vital to the war effort
could not enlist
he pulled muck
but wanted to fly

the old-timers
still talk of my aunt
in the mine
during the war
outmucking the men

the motorman
on the ore train goes home
to his shotgun —
his youngest son
never the same

Muck is the earth and rock material produced by blasting in a mine. *Mucking* is the process of removing this material for processing at a smelter.

A *motorman* was the driver of an electric engine on an ore train. Like streetcars, these engines were powered from overhead cables.

on the casket
of one miner
a wreath
cedar boughs from camp
woven by his wife

expecting
their second child
long outgrown
the cramped quarters
of the bunkhouse

at the gate
union organizers recruit
miners
the company stops repairs
to their housing

the smokestack
exhales 24/7
imagine
the profits singing
red hot in that smelter

exposed
by an early fall
behind the foliage
a blue-green tailings pond
where nothing grows

so familiar
dad's mining clothes
all those years
I never saw him
wear them

forty-three years
working underground
buried
in a job he hated...
evening Bible studies

his religious texts
ranked between
my bookends
cut and polished chunks
of Sudbury Breccia

Haiku / Senryu
I I I

the rattlesnake
unseen until it moves —
heat of August

high noon...
the geraniums
shout red

August moon
somewhere in the dark
a blues harp

scent of pine...
the summer moon
rocking on a bough

hitting my fly
just above the ripples
late season walleye

March break…
the exquisite sting
of the man-o'-war

deer antlers
among new ferns
— fire season

spring rain
out of dark earth
the reddest radish

after the flood
jazz licks
on rusted trombones

AC/DC
my heart beating
with the kick drum

heat lightning
the chirr of crickets
at dusk

first tomato
mother picks for me
the sun's warmth

field tent at dusk
sharing pumpernickel
with snapping turtles

fossil hunting —
under a flat sun-baked slab
a coiled black racer

cornflower blue
among crickets and tall grass
centrosaur bones

infant death...
looking for a lighter shade
of blue

June sun —
chilled to the marrow
from the morgue

thinning the carrots...
still thinking about the child
miscarried

wilted
waiting for the rain
me and the green beans

overgrown lot
alive with grasshoppers
— distant thunder

double rainbow
her second wish
a small one

the last fresh corn —
incoming fog
lopping the trees

the sound of oars
directionless in the fog
— thermos of cocoa

September moon
sweetness of the last
honeysuckle

the tiny finch…
glimpses of yellow
in poplar greens

sun on water
the graceful whip
of the fly rod

cold rain
all at once
the leaves let go

cremated
in his faded jeans
— new leaf blower

brisk autumn breeze
a flash of panties
on the bus steps

full bus
breathing each other's breath
frosted windows

snowy night —
waiting for father's breath,
I hold mine

more snow coming —
cougar prints parallel
the deer tracks

orienteers
under stars, under snow
under eider

deep winter
the golden crust of cheese
on onion soup

windchill warning
car seats cold and stiff
Preparation H

March wind
the buzz
of flaking paint

flaky yellow paint
on the old lamp post —
van of giggly girls

blood-orange sun
distant pines
a jagged black line

ax wedged
in the chopping block —
sunset silhouettes

night
takes the distant pines
first

poplar saplings
grown through a burnt-out
Model A

the backyard
after the funeral —
aspen in bud

mother's grave
her Polish niece takes home
a bit of earth

cactus flowers...
dinosaur footprints in shale

spring garden...
not knowing when to stop

pick-ur-own farm...
can't resist
pulling a few weeds

brook trout
waving with the current
spring bear hunt

roofless cabin
where the river bends
hiss of the fly reel

buzz of cicadas...
to be that fern
by the cool stream

the taste of stick
after the Popsicle…
sweltering

cherry tomatoes
cradled in my hands
August heat

harvest
'round the clock
— dust and diesel

this fall
the oleander left outdoors
mother's dreams

stripped of leaves
poplars in the cold wind...
pot of tea brewing

first snow
the dog lifts her paws
higher

winter gale
water in the basement
IV stopped flowing

cold out there
the dog allowed
on the sofa

nodding
over my steamy broth
endless winter

March storm —
the snowbanks
white again

freezing rain
the dead air sound
of the empty house

moving day —
she wants to take the garden
with her

dad's workbench
the lawn mower repair
he'll never finish

after his stroke
  radishes
    going to seed

        second summer
        the candle she lights
        when it gets bad

                    campsite sounds
                    her wet swimsuit
                    see-through

        shorter days
        tomato suckers
        left unpinched

fall camp sale
the frayed cowhide jacket
that feels like dad

the shriveled surface
of a neglected grapefruit
dusting of snow

Christmas Eve
frozen turkey dinner
for one

Mother's Day:
my son serves the takeout
on china

spring cleaning
finally letting go
of dad's wardrobe

his unwelcome scent
on her spring jacket
the cat hisses

shirtsleeves
the bag lady's smile
full of rotted teeth

thin cotton dress as I walk I shrink into myself

two teenage girls
kissing at the bus stop
summer rockfest

hot with color
peony petals
cool to my nose

crack in the sidewalk
defined by clumps of grass
a dandelion

dog days
the damp dishcloth
begins to smell

new dog
calling him
by the old one's name

junkyard fence —
barking guard dogs
barking shins

old bush road
among the ostrich ferns
crumbling tires

gulls like decoys
on a warm asphalt sea
— first raindrop

fall mist...
the buzz and flicker
of the motel's 'M'

colder days...
behind the plow
furrows white with gulls

prospective son-in-law
the farmer notes
the boy's smooth white hands

chill March wind
if only I could say
what I really think

Christmas dinner
discussing why our family
finds farts so funny

the gibbous moon
impaled on the church spire
Shrove Tuesday

clouds touching clouds
a lamb nuzzles
its mother

barbecued ribs
my three-year-old tries to touch
the bumblebee

bumblebees —
faded blue coaster bike
against the garage

blue asters...
father's eyes
no longer know me

winter solstice
only our shadows
touch

tea kettle
boiling itself dry
ambulance

insomnia
three a.m. donuts
with the cops

winter night...
father's last words
never come

freezing rain...
snowbanks turn a darker shade
of white

dad's fedora
as if he were still here
autumn again

withered juniper
mother's hair
since the nursing home

November rain
the jack-o'-lantern's
moldy grin

Tanka

fortunate I am
to have loved twice
sadly
my wife was not
one of them

box by box
parents' possessions
discarded
in my heart I keep
the broken wedding vows

later
under the influence
I wavered
almost asked you back
luckily, the morphine wore off

you ask why
I don't write about you
    take comfort
        you don't cause
           that kind of pain

evenings
now that you are gone
I find
the house strangely quiet
and oh so peaceful

as a child
I wanted to touch the sky
never dreaming
that to touch another's heart
would be the greater challenge

she is crying
something I said
or should have said
perhaps it's just
that time of month

radiant
bursting with her news
she's pregnant
not a good time
to say I'm leaving

two a.m.
she can't stop crying
two weeks now
she got rid of both
father and fetus

at thirty
her daughter questions
an abortion clinic
appointment card
from twenty years ago

watching
leaves on the wind
hand on my belly
a week
since the last kick

no heartbeat
on the ultrasound –
tonight my heart
is a ragged wound
beating without reason

home again
after the stillbirth
howling
in the shower until
the hot water runs out

my child's death
I plant dwarf delphiniums
needing
that shade of blue
to lighten my heart

in the lunchroom
a woman knits baby clothes
closing my eyes
I rest my hands
on my flat, flat belly

missing
from the CV's stark facts
of my life
ten lost years
trying to have a child

in dad's box
of old receipts
thirty-year-old
hospital parking stub
the day she was born

my three-year-old
oblivious to all but
her Legos
morning coffee
before my first class

giggling
she blows the pinwheel
too quickly
our weekend together
is over

watching
her grandchildren play
in the plastic pool
beaches a jumble of
tsunami victims

with her son
waiting for the school bus
half-smiling
knowing soon
he won't want her there

down the street
two teenaged boys
shooting hoops
the sound of impact
out of sync with the bounce

at the mall entrance
my teenager edges away
for now
I am not
his mother

that barbecue
leaning over the railing
talking
your floppy neckline
and braless young breasts

in her future
tall, dark, handsome
oncologist
who would tell her
she has no future

the energy
of the morning sun
recharging
my weakened body
and my triple As

my daily walk
an encounter with
relativity
somehow the same distance
continues to get longer

each day
we pass in the street
and smile 'hi'
          sometimes I find her
          walking through my thoughts

not enough butt
to fill my underwear
I am so thin
my Tilley hat makes me
look like a roofing nail

short of breath
walking into the wind
gale-force gusts
overwhelming the efforts
of my oxygen tank

reduced to reading
cereal boxes
no books
shut-in service and I
wait out the snow

ezine launch
reading her poetry
on Skype
finally I put a face
to my email friend

the second hand
on my watch mirrors
my life
long periods of stasis
between jerks

my bad day
brought into perspective
I watch
the ambulance
pull in next door

suddenly
awake in the dark
gasping
afraid it won't stop
more afraid it will

at the ER
I am assumed senile
the nurse
directs her questions
to my young driver

country DJ
from my parents' room
camouflage
to mask sounds
of more intimate music

the others
off to midnight Mass
in the dark
Basil Rathbone reads
Masque of the Red Death

furiously
I deadhead Shasta daisies
to prolong summer
clip old lady bristles
off my chin

my face
in the mirror
age spots
outnumber freckles
...summer's touch fading

evening
sensing eyes on me
I look up
from my crossword puzzle
to find you smiling

elderly neighbors
argue over stray garbage –
without warning
    go back where ya came from,
    ya fuckin' Polack

        from my cousin
        dried boletus mushrooms
        intense and earthy
        the aroma of my parents'
        Polish homeland

      father
      in the nursing home
        ever smaller
          the circles he walks
          the circles of his thoughts

Boletus edulis is a highly prized European wild mushroom, aka *porcini* or *cepes,* considered the king of wild mushrooms in Poland.

a tireless source
of Great Depression tales
my dad
cannot remember
if he ate breakfast

he swears
there will be no dignity
the reaper
will have to take him
kicking and screaming

for the first time
since I was a child
I hold dad's hand
praying he will rally
know his hand is in mine

mom's notes
from the hospital
prayer cards
pain too great to write
more than a few lines

no coffin,
just laid out on a gurney
under a quilt…
you'd be so proud to know
I didn't waste a penny

dad's fedora
stored in the closet
too damned big
I never did
measure up

at the mirror
talking to myself
dad's voice
ten years now
he hasn't used it

only now
after mother's passing
do I let
my hair grow long
wear my heart on my sleeve

your apron
still behind the kitchen door –
how much
I want to forget
you were my mother

her compliments
pinched pennies
from a thin, thin wallet...
the kindest words
leave me cold

my husband gone
my friends gone now, too...
arms outstretched
I am a stick figure
on this whirling planet

the March wind
blows raw and cold
at my front door
an earnest young couple
leaflets from God in hand

he denies
the similarities
between
the distortions of Dali
and those of his faith

near the end
dad apologizes
somehow
with time passed
a nonissue

I rest my paddle
let the canoe drift awhile
rocks   trees   sky
the lake and I
are an empty mirror

Haibun

Tarpaper Shack

Ignatius Fay

My father lived in a tarpaper shack with his mother, three sisters and two brothers through the Great Depression. His father was a lumberjack and an alcoholic, seldom home.

The shack sweltered in the summer. Two bedrooms upstairs, a kitchen and living area on the ground floor, it had no insulation, just tarred paper over wood held in place by narrow laths. Doors and windows were opened to allow air to circulate and the family spent a lot of time outdoors. Most of the cooking was done on a small wood stove under a lean-to outside.

Winters were brutal and the shack became an ice locker. The only heat came from the wood stove in the kitchen. Moisture from cooking and human bodies formed a six-inch-thick pillar of ice, ceiling to floor, in the northwest corner. The second floor was abandoned and everyone slept huddled on the main floor.

between me
and Jack Frost
two panes of glass

Uncle Peter

Ignatius Fay

Foxhole in France.

Night lit by distant artillery.

He and his partner huddled, smoking, talking softly.

Lookouts alert for advancing German infantry.

Orders to engage and hold the line.

Taking turns peering over the rim of the foxhole.

Scanning the area for movement.

His turn.

A couple of faraway explosions light the horizon, casting shadows.

Nothing moving.

Turning back in time to see his buddy's headless torso pitch forward.

Reflex.

Reaching to grab him.

Missing his grip.

Missing his right arm from just below the elbow.

Pain coming later.

electric wheelchair
flying Canadian flags
'don't walk' light

Pets-des-sœurs

Ignatius Fay

Mom is making pies. I notice she consistently rolls her crusts quite a bit bigger than needed, leaving a lot of overlap to trim. The remnants she puts off to the side.

"Mom, if you used a little less dough, you'd have less waste when you trim your pies."

She smiles. "Don't you like *Pets-des-sœurs?*"

This pastry is made by buttering a flattened portion of dough, covering it with brown sugar and cinnamon, and rolling it into a fat cigar shape. Cut into one-inch-thick pinwheels, it is baked on a cookie sheet. We savor these treats, slowly unwinding the coil, while giggling at the English name—Nuns' Farts!

"Mom! You know I love them!"

"Well, they were invented as a way of using up leftover pie dough. You're not supposed to use fresh dough. So, the less leftover dough, the fewer *Pets-des-sœurs.*"

lost in the snow
no stone on her grave
all these years

Responsibility

Ignatius Fay

He was—
      a math whiz
      an eager student
      a music lover
      a drummer in a band
      a fine tenor
      an exceptional jitterbugger
      the oldest of eleven
      the son of a drunk

The Great Depression: To help his mother, he quit school in Grade 11 to work in the logging camps. It was a job and she had a lot of mouths to feed.

World War II: The war effort needed miners. He was helping his country. Besides, the pay was better and he wanted to get married. He hated mining, but it was a job.

The fifties: He got his chance to sing professionally. By now, he had a wife and three children. The risk was too great and he couldn't do that to his family.

The sixties: After his wife died, leaving him with five children, he panicked. He couldn't raise them properly on his own. His new wife was a widow with three children, essentially doubling his burden.

The later years: At the camp, he only swam after dusk to wash up. Between the house and the new cottage, renovation projects and maintenance, he had a lot of demands on his time. He retired after forty-one years in the mines, having hated every minute.

He died at seventy-eight, a cynical, unhappy, but responsible man.

spring convocation
I finally tell dad
he's full of it

Cleaning the Church

Ignatius Fay

A small volunteer group shares responsibilities for cleaning the church in the evenings. When it is my dad's month, I go with him. I redistribute the hymnals, raise all the kneelers, pick up loose trash, sweep, mop and, lately, polish the floor. Man, I love using that big electric polisher, although it is not always easy to tell which of us is in control!

The best part of the evening is walking to and from the church. We go right after supper and, being winter, it is already dark. We walk down the center of the street following the wheel ruts in four inches of snow, large flakes falling through the glow of the street lights. In our small town, traffic is sparse and we are in no danger. We talk about family matters, about school, or sometimes he grills me in my multiplication tables. The topic isn't important. It is just great to be the two of us walking and talking.

cold snap
asleep on the last pew
the local wino

Once

Ignatius Fay

Dad and I went to see her in the hospital for the weekend. Man, was she burnt! And in agony. At home, she had been in pain for some time. Dad had moved her into my bed and me to the couch because she could not sleep with him. Many afternoons I came in from school to be greeted by her moans and cries of pain from my room upstairs.

Saturday afternoon we took a walk, just the two of us. She was visibly struggling with something she wanted to say. Finally, 'I hope that someday, when you are older, you'll understand. I can't take this anymore. The pain is too much. I have no fight left. I am giving up.' She never took another radiation treatment.

The next Thursday, late in the afternoon, my aunt came to find me on the ball field. Gently, in somber tones, she gave me the news, then escorted me home. No tears. On the way, a friend yelled from up the street, did I want to go over and play? 'No, I have to go home. My mother is dead.' No tears.

Through the preparations, the days of visitation, all the visitors and condolences, the funeral and the interment, no tears. Dad and my sisters cried almost nonstop.

After supper on a beautiful autumn evening two weeks later, I was playing chess with a friend on his porch steps. His parents were enjoying coffee and chatting on the porch above us. Out of nowhere, it hit me. Never again would I sit on the porch in the evening with my mother!

And the tears came. That once.

It was 1961 and I was eleven.

her blue budgie
mute in her absence
shorter days

Atonement

Ignatius Fay

In Grade 11, I spend six months as a custom-order thief to make spending money. Until the thought: "What are you doing? This is wrong and you know it."

By my calculation, I have stolen about $185 in merchandise from the same store, a lot of money in 1966. Determined to repay the money, I start shoveling driveways—lots of takers because I do a very good job. When summer comes, I mow lawns, despite being allergic to cut grass. I take a lot of medication!

One fall day, on the way home from school, I stop to see the manager in his office. Explaining, I hand over the money with apologies. He thanks me, but says he can't commend me for correcting a situation I should not have created in the first place.

The corporation probably will never see that money. But that's his moral baggage, isn't it?

on the sill
stealing red from the sun
green tomatoes

Impromptu Visit

Ignatius Fay

My wife and I are entertaining two young couples in our new house. One of the guys pulls out a new 8mm porn flick and, in short order, the wall of the living room is writhing with images of sex. The doorbell rings. It's Aunty Rita, a nun, in full habit.

"I was in the area and thought I'd stop and say hello, maybe get a look at your new home. I hope I'm not interrupting."

"No, no. We're just sitting around watching a porn movie."

My wife turns beet red. "As if you just say that to a nun. What will she think!"

Aunty Rita is pretty 'together.' She just laughs and asks, "Are they any good?" Her quick tour of the house finishes just as her ride returns.

"Do you watch a lot of porno films? I can put you in contact with a good supplier. His prices are quite reasonable."

Our friend thanks her for the offer, but assures her that he doesn't.

"Well, if you change your mind, have my nephew get hold of me." And she is gone.

beyond the backyard
acres of flowering spuds
dogs running free

Postpartum

Irene Golas

His eyes tell me all I need to know. The news is bad, so bad he can't look at me. Wishes he were anywhere but here. Here, a hospital room. He, a doctor delivering the news. My baby just died.

I can't breathe...can't speak. Can't do anything except lock eyes on his. Every particle is frozen...motionless. I see his lips move. Hear the word 'dead.' See him turn and hurry from the room.

Down the hall, a baby—someone else's baby—starts to cry. Hot knife through ice. Every cell a searing scream...

raw wind
I touch my child's name
on the gravestone

Christmas Magic

Irene Golas

Christmas coming! Mother and Father talking about Santa. How he'll come early Christmas morning, leave lots of presents and candy under the tree.

Down the chimney, Mother says.

Won't he get dirty? (I've seen Father cleaning the stovepipes. *Don't touch the soot! Poison!*)

Soot doesn't bother Santa, he's *magic.* What would you like him to bring?

Licorice and toffee and storybooks, a great big teddy bear and a doll with blue eyes.

Only if you're good, you know. The bad kids—he leaves rocks in their socks. Try putting those on.

Oh, I'll be good! I promise. I'll tell him myself.

No, no! Won't come unless you're asleep—can't be seen.

Just a *peek?*

He's an elf—extra keen senses. He'll go pop! Disappear.

What's he look like?

Old, they say. Dressed in red, sack of presents on his back. Should leave him a treat, he works so hard.

Cookies!

Good idea. We'll make them together.

Rum! Father says. It's cold driving a sleigh all night.

Let's give him both.

Both! Yes, that's my girl!

Don't forget the reindeer, Mother says. They get hungry flying all over with that heavy sleigh.

Do they really fly? How?

Magic. Only way Santa can get to every house on Christmas Eve.

Can we give them apples? Mr. Dunnagan, he gives apples to his horses.

They'll like apples, I'm sure. Haven't any at the North Pole—all ice and snow. That's where Santa lives.

Why?

No more questions, Mother laughs. Off to bed. Tomorrow we've work to do—lots of baking.

And get us a Christmas tree, Father says. The biggest we can find. Here's a kiss good night. Sweet dreams, princess.

December evening
the smell of gingerbread
in mother's hug

Streamers

Ignatius Fay

My heart has me in the ER on New Year's Eve. At 2:30 a.m., a girl in her late teens is brought in, unconscious, and placed two cubicles from mine. Her parents and her boyfriend are given chairs along the wall.

A nurse takes information. The parents know only that their daughter went to a party with her boyfriend. Three long, colored streamers still hang around his neck. He describes a drinking game gone bad, his girlfriend losing consciousness and his calling 911.

An hour later, the doctor declares the girl dead of alcohol poisoning. He signs some forms and leaves. By five o'clock, the cubicle is empty save for a skewed, rumpled bed and three well-trampled party streamers on the floor.

shaky signatures
on the donor forms –
windchill

Pollution

Ignatius Fay

Not that old, really, he walks the same route at the same time each day carrying his oxygen tank. His wide-brimmed Tilley on his head and aided by a gnarled walking stick almost thicker than he is, he has become a fixture on the street these past twenty-five years. Anyone who uses that thoroughfare in mid-afternoon has come to expect him.

He suffers from lung and, now, heart disease and should be long dead. Twenty-five years ago, when they removed most of his left lung, they said the disease would kill him within four years. His response was to ask what he could do to maximize his stay on the planet. They told him.

And damned if he didn't go home and do what they told him to do! And he continues to do it.

So, he walks every day. He carries a net cloth bag attached to his tank with a carabiner. As he encounters them, he slowly and carefully bends to pick up recyclable pieces of trash and stuffs them in his bag. He pauses at the bus stops to empty his bag into the appropriate recycling bins. He believes if you are not part of the solution, you are part of the pollution.

huge iguana
draped over his shoulder
waiting for the bus

(arising from a comment made by Andrea Pellerin)

A Note about the Authors

Irene Golas discovered the world of haiku when she purchased a slender volume of Japanese nature poetry in a gift shop in Elmvale, Ontario. Her first haiku were published in 2005, followed by her first tanka in 2006. Her poems have appeared in many print and online journals, as well as in a number of anthologies.

Ignatius Fay is a retired invertebrate paleontologist who has been writing haiku and related forms of poetry for more than twenty years. Writing primarily for his own pleasure and as a means of personal expression, he didn't submit his work for publication until 2008, the year of his first published poem. Since then, his poems have been published in many of the most respected print and online journals.

In 2008, he published a small book of haiku/senryu, *Haiga Moments: pens and lens,* with photographs by Ray Belcourt, of Leduc, Alberta. In 2011, he published *Points In Between,* an anecdotal history of his early years.

Both authors reside in Sudbury, Ontario.

Publication Credits

Irene Golas

Acorn: 'the dog's shadow' 'heat wave' – no. 14, Spring 2005; 'the fetus kicks just twice' 'high noon' 'winter solstice' – no. 19, Fall 2007; 'parsley' – no. 21, Fall 2008; **American Tanka:** 'watching' – issue 15/16, 2006; **bottle rockets:** 'autumn rain' 'clouds touching clouds' 'first tomato' – vol. 8, no. 1 (#15), 2006; **Eucalypt:** 'no heartbeat' – issue 1, November 2006; 'box by box' – issue 3, November 2007; 'only now' – issue 4, Spring 2008; 'as a child' – issue 7, Fall 2009; **Frogpond:** 'home again' – vol. XXVIII, no. 2, Spring/Summer 2005; 'smokehouse embers' – vol. XXX, no. 3, Fall 2007; **Haiku Canada Review:** 'every step through creaking snow' – vol. 1, no. 1, February 2007; 'nursing home' – vol. 2, no. 2, October 2008; **Haiku Canada Sheets:** 'sudden shower' – HCS 2004-2005, Honorable Mention, The Betty Drevniok Award, 2004; 'first warm day' – HCS 2007-2008, Honorable Mention, The Betty Drevniok Award, 2007; **The Heron's Nest:** 'autumn sunset' – vol. VII, no. 3, September 2005; 'cherry tomatoes' – vol. VIII, no. 2, June 2006; 'thinning the carrots' – vol. VIII, no. 4, December 2006; 'winter night' – vol. IX, no. 3, September 2007; 'withered juniper' – vol. X, no. 4, December 2008; **HighGrader:** 'Christmas Magic' – December 2007; **Lyrical Passion Poetry E-Zine:** 'lilac on the breeze' – 2nd place, 2010 Haiku Pen Contest [in slightly different form]; 'moss-covered rocks' – 1st place, 2010 Haiku Pen Contest; 'no coffin' – Honorable Mention, 2010 Think TANKA Contest; **Multiverses:** 'furiously' 'the March wind' 'missing' – 1.1, 2012; **Northern Ontario Poetry Collections:** 'hearse and two limos' 'March storm' 'summer evening' – Ten Pines, vol. 10, 2005; 'hot night' 'long johns' – Sylvan Jottings, vol. 11, 2006; **red lights:** 'for the first time' 'home again' – vol. 8, no. 2, June 2012; **Ribbons:** 'in the lunchroom' 'my husband gone' – vol. 6, no. 1, Spring 2010; **Roadrunner:** 'mother's funeral' 'postpartum' – August 2005, issue V:3; **Shamrock:** 'new dog' – no. 18, Spring 2011; **Shiki Monthly Kukai:** 'Mother's Day' – 1st place, July 2005; 'farmers' market' – 1st place, December 2005; 'hunter's moon' – September 2006; 'box of crayons' – December 2006 [in slightly different form]; 'double rainbow' – 3rd place, September 2007; 'deep winter' – December 2007; 'days grow short' – 2nd place, January 2008 [in slightly different form]; 'blue asters' – March 2008; *Simply Haiku:* 'cumulus clouds' 'first snow' 'hanging laundry' 'snow falling' – vol. 3, no. 4, Winter 2005; 'Postpartum' – vol. 4, no. 4, Winter 2006; 'after his stroke' 'November rain' 'overnight' – vol. 5, no. 3, Autumn 2007; *Sulphur:* 'the smokestack' – issue 1, Spring 2011; 'Greyhound west' – issue 2, Spring 2012; *Tanka Splendor 2006:* 'father'; *terra north/nord:* 'bone-snapping cold' 'the earth rumbles' 'Junction Creek' 'nickel town' 'no more blueberries' – vol. 1, issue 1, Fall 2010; 'bush, rocks and water' 'cold out there' 'freezing rain' 'moving day' 'scent of pine' 'spring thaw' – vol. 1, issue 2, Spring 2011; 'I rest my paddle' – vol. 1, issue 3, Summer 2011; *The Touch of a Moth:* 'cancer' – Haiku Canada Anthology, 35th Anniversary Edition, May 2012; *World Haiku Review:* 'about the war' (Editor's Choice; also 1st place, Shintai); 'snowy night' (Honorable Mention, Neo-Classic); 'autumn wind' 'bone scan' 'dementia ward' – vol. 6, issue 3, May 2008

Ignatius Fay

bottle rockets: 'riverside park' – vol. 13, no. 2 (#26), 2012; *Chrysanthemum:* 'fortunate am I' – issue 11, April 2012; *Concise Delight:* 'hitting my fly' – vol. 2, 2009; *Daily Haiga:* 'harvest' 'lobster traps' 'Valentine's Day' – December 2010; *Frogpond:* 'Atonement' 'Responsibility' – vol. XXXV, no. 2, Spring/Summer 2012; *Haigaonline:* 'by lamplight' – December 2011; 'the shriveled surface' 'through her reflection'– March 2012; *Haiku Canada Holographic Anthology:* 'wilted' – May 2012; *Haiku Canada Review:* 'fossil hunting' – Fall 2009; 'gunmetal blue' – Winter/ Spring 2011; *The Heron's Nest:* 'cool March breeze' – vol. XI, no. 2, 2009; 'the dog and I' – vol. XI, no. 3, 2009; 'worlds apart' – vol. XII, no. 3, 2010; 'dog days' – vol. XIII, no. 3, 2011; *in the clear dawn sky:* 'the backyard' – Haiku Canada Anthology, 2008–2009; *Lyrical Passion Poetry E-zine:* 'flannel p.j.s' – Honorable Mention, 2011 Haiku Pen Contest; *Modern Haiku:* 'more snow coming' – 42.1, Winter/ Spring 2011; 'hummingbird' – 42.3, Fall 2011; *Multiverses:* 'evenings' 'in her future' 'sun on water' 'too normal' – 1.1, 2012; **Notes From the Gean:** 'her brother's hug' 'insomnia' – vol 2, issue 3, December 2010; 'deep red cranberries' 'jar of skin creme' 'meteor shower' 'note from mom' – vol. 3, issue 1, June 2011; **Observer Observed:** 'Christmas Day' – Haiku Canada Anthology, 2011; **red lights:** 'at the mirror' – vol. 8, no. 2, June 2012; **Shamrock:** 'March wind' – no. 18, 2011; 'Pollution' – no. 20, 2011; **Shiki Monthly Kukai:** 'August moon' – tied for first place, August 2010; **Sketchbook:** 'crack in the sidewalk' 'throat-searing heat' – July/August 2009; 'basting the turkey' 'cool fingertips' 'the sound of oars' – September/October 2009; 'cheery bouquet' 'dried forget-me-nots' 'freezing rain' 'morning stiffness' 'the rattlesnake' – March/ April 2011; **Sulphur:** 'office picnic' 'Stanley Cup game' – issue 1, Spring 2011; 'not enough butt' 'on the wall' 'Once' 'under the eaves' – issue 2, Spring 2012; **terra north/nord:** 'rain day at camp' – vol. 1, issue 2, 2011; 'cross-tie walking' 'first cattails' – vol. 1, issue 3, 2011; 'mom's notes' – vol. 1, issue 4, 2011; **A Thousand Gourds:** 'absences' 'Day of the Dead' 'fall camp sale' – December 2011; **World Haiku Review:** 'diagnosis' (Haiku of Merit, General); 'idling tour bus' (Haiku of Merit, Shintai); 'mid-January' (Haiku of Merit, General); 'so much to be said' (Honorable Mention, Shintai); 'weathered old man' (Honorable Mention, Neo-Classic) – August 2010